PHYSICS
Experiments
for Children

Formerly titled SCIENCE FOR CHILDREN

by Muriel Mandell

Illustrated by S. Matsuda

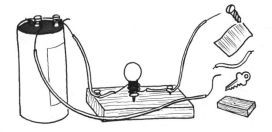

Dover Publications, Inc., New York

CONTENTS

Published in Canada by General Publishing Company, Ltd.,
30 Lesmill Road, Don Mills, Toronto, Ontario
Published in the United Kingdom by Constable and Company, Ltd.,
10 Orange Street, London WC 2.

This Dover edition, first published in 1968, is an unabridged
and unaltered republication of the work originally published in
1959 under the title *Science for Children*. The work is reprinted
by special arrangement with Sterling Publishing Company, Inc..
publisher of the original edition.

Standard Book Number: 486-22033-8
Library of Congress Catalog Card Number: 68-9308

Manufactured in the United States of America
Dover Publications, Inc.
180 Varick Street
New York, N. Y. 10014

To Mark and Jonathan and all the other children
who ask why

INTRODUCTION

Science is a way of looking at things, a way of questioning and of figuring out answers by thinking, by trying them out (experimenting), and by reading about other people's experiences and experiments.

A scientist is a person who tries to understand and to find the answers to some of our questions about the physical world.

You too can be a scientist. To begin, don't take everything for granted. Start to question the world around you by performing the experiments in this book.

Set aside a special corner or shelf for your odds and ends of equipment. Ordinary shoeboxes make good storage bins.

You can perform the experiments safely by following directions and using simple care. (You can get burnt by drinking an ordinary cup of hot chocolate carelessly!) The experiments on electricity call for the use of storage batteries or dry cells. It is never necessary and it is dangerous to use house current. If you are not yet able to cook an egg over the stove, ask an older friend or adult to help you with those few experiments that require a candle or other source of heat. Always keep a basin of cold water handy.

If an experiment fails to work, try it again—and find out why it failed the first time. Sometimes you can learn more from failure than from success.

While you may start with an experiment from any chapter, it is best to concentrate on one chapter at a time and perform most of the experiments, preferably in the order given, before you go on to another topic. The experiments are not meant to be tricks with which to amaze yourself and your friends (though they may do that, too!), but to provide experiences and to illustrate scientific principles. The world of fact, you will find, can be more exciting than the world of fancy.

1. MATTER: AIR

DOES AIR TAKE UP SPACE?

Stuff a large handkerchief or some crumpled newspaper into an empty glass or jar. Make sure the handkerchief won't fall out when you turn the glass upside down.

Then, fill a pot with water. Holding the glass so that its mouth is down, put the glass deep into the pot of water and hold it there. After a minute or two, pull the glass out of the water and remove the handkerchief.

You will see that: The handkerchief is dry.

Explanation: Water cannot fill the glass because the glass is already filled with air. The "empty" glass is full of air. So, air takes up space.

Air is a gas. It has no size or shape of its own but will fill every space it can.

Place a funnel in the neck of an empty soda bottle. Pack clay around the neck of the bottle so that there is no space between the bottle and the funnel.

Pour water into the funnel. Notice what happens.

Then take the clay off the bottle and funnel.

You will see that: While the clay is there, the water remains in the funnel or enters the bottle only in slow spurts. When the clay is removed, the water flows freely into the bottle.

Explanation: The clay seals the neck of the bottle outside of the funnel. When water flows into the funnel, the air cannot escape except by going through the water very slowly. The air in the bottle takes up space and prevents the water from coming in. When the clay is removed and air is able to leave around the neck of the bottle, then water can flow in. This proves that air takes up space.

DOES AIR WEIGH ANYTHING?

Drill holes (or make notches) 6 inches from each end of a narrow 3-foot length of wood, such as a yardstick. Then, make a hole in the exact center of the stick, 18 inches from each end. Place a cord or wire through the center hole and suspend the stick from a chair back or a rod.

Blow up a large balloon or beach ball. Tie its mouth tight and hang it from one of the end holes of the stick. Then, suspend a small can or box (such as a baking powder container) from the other hole. (See illustration.) Put a little sand or rice in the can until the stick balances.

Then, let the air out of the balloon.

You will see that: The can sinks down as the air is let out of the balloon.

Explanation: When the air leaves the balloon, the balloon becomes lighter. Air has weight.

At sea level, air weighs 1¼ ounces per cubic foot. (See if you can find a carton, or stack up books, to measure 1 foot wide, 1 foot long and 1 foot deep. Then you will know the space taken up by 1¼ ounces of air.) On a mountaintop, air is a little thinner and weighs less.

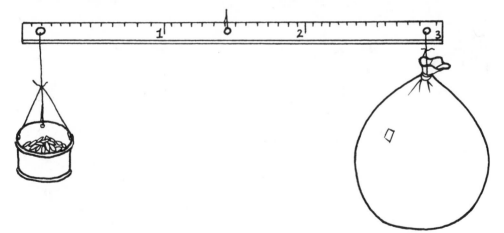

WHICH IS HEAVIER,
HOT AIR OR COLD?

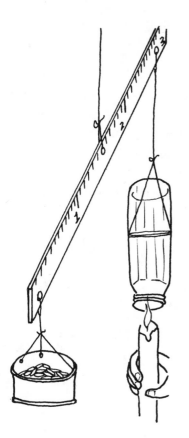

Balance an "empty" baby bottle on one end of your yardstick and a tin can on the other. Put sand or rice in the can if needed.

Hold a candle flame for one minute near the mouth of the bottle. Remove the flame and balance the scale again.

You will see that: The bottle goes up when heat is applied to the air in it. You must remove sand or rice from the can on the other end to balance the scale.

Explanation: Warm air weighs less than cold air occupying the same space.

WHAT HAPPENS TO WARM AIR?

Rinse one jar with very cold water, and rinse another jar with hot water. Dry them both thoroughly.

With a cardboard between them, place the jars mouth to mouth with the warm jar on the bottom. Ask someone to blow a puff of cigarette smoke into the bottom bottle, as you lift the cardboard. Let the smoke fill the bottom jar, and then pull out the cardboard.

You will see that: The smoke will rise from the lower to the upper jar.

Explanation: The smoke rises as the warm light air rises and the cold heavier air sinks.

Try the experiment with the cold jar on the bottom and the warm one on top. What happens this time?

AIR PRESSES
IN ALL DIRECTIONS

WHAT IS WIND?

Sprinkle talcum powder on a cloth. Shake a little of the powder off near a lamp with a light bulb which is not lighted. Notice what happens to the powder.

Then light the bulb and give it a few minutes to get hot. Shake some more powder off the cloth.

You will see that: Before the bulb is turned on, the powder sinks slowly down through the air. After the bulb is hot, the powder rises.

Explanation: When the air gets warmed by the lighted bulb, it rises, carrying the lightweight talcum powder with it. The cooler heavier air is pushed down.

This flowing of cooler air to take the place of hot air happens outdoors too. We know it as wind.

Cover the wide mouth of a funnel with a piece of rubber from a balloon or from a rubber sheet. Tie the rubber on tightly.

Suck some air from the narrow end of the funnel and notice what happens to the rubber. Turn the funnel upside down and suck in again. Then turn the funnel sideways and suck in.

You will see that: When you suck in the air, the rubber is pulled in. The same thing happens whatever the direction of the funnel.

Explanation: You are removing air from the inside of the funnel by sucking in. The outside push of air is then greater than the

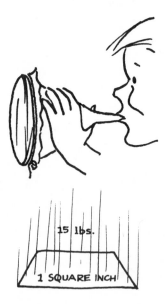

push inside, even when the funnel is held upside down or sideways. Air pushes equally in all directions.

The push—or pressure—of air is almost 15 pounds per square inch at sea level. (There are 15 pounds of air pressing on this picture of a square inch.)

CAN AIR HOLD UP WATER?

Fill a glass or jar with water. Place a piece of cardboard or stiff paper on top of the glass. Hold the cardboard in place and turn the glass upside down over a sink or basin. Then take your hand away from the cardboard.

You will see that: The water stays in the glass until the cardboard becomes soaked.

Explanation: The water is held in the glass because of the pressure of air outside the glass against the cardboard. This air pressure is greater than the pressure of water against the cardboard.

If the experiment doesn't work the first time, try again. This time, fill the glass to the very brim and make sure no bubble of air enters between the cardboard and glass as you turn the glass over.

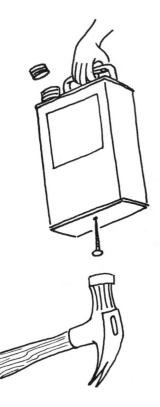

A TRICK BOTTLE

Punch a small hole near the bottom of an empty can that has a screw top (a floor-wax can, for instance).

Fill the can with water and cap it quickly. Notice what happens. Then remove the top.

You will see that: As long as the top is on, the water will not flow from the hole. When you take off the top, the water flows freely.

Explanation: Air presses up harder than the water presses down until you remove the top. Then the air pressure on top plus the pressure of the water make the downward pressure greater.

HOW DOES A STRAW WORK?

Color a few ounces of water with vegetable dye. Place a paper or glass straw in a glass with the colored water. Suck up a little of the water into the straw. Then hold your finger across the top of the straw and pull the straw out of the liquid. What happens?

Then remove your finger from the top of the straw.

You will see that: While your finger covers the top of the straw, the liquid remains in the straw. When you remove the finger, the water flows out.

Explanation: With your finger you are lessening the pressure of air over the straw. The greater pressure of air under the straw can hold the liquid inside the straw.

HOW DO SUCTION CUPS WORK?

You will need two sink plungers for this experiment. Ask a friend to bring a sink plunger from his kitchen when he comes to visit you. Using your own, too, press the cups together. Now try to separate them. Each of you can pull hard.

You will see that: It takes great effort to separate the plungers.

Press one of the plungers against a smooth kitchen chair. Try to lift it. *You will see that*: The chair can be lifted with the plunger.

Explanation: You have forced out the air from the inside of the plunger and thus reduced the air pressure from within. The pressure from the outside is then more powerful. Suction is actually a difference in air pressures.

Now you know why suction-capped arrows stick to a smooth board or wall.

Try to press a suction cup to a window screen or to a grate. Why doesn't it hold?

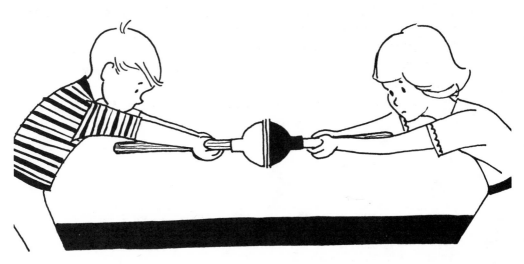

THE SIPHON

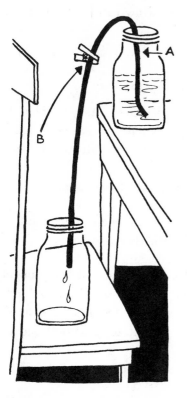

Place a tall jar almost full of water on the table and an empty jar of about the same size on a chair alongside the table. Fill a rubber tube or shower hose with water and hold the water in by pinching both ends of the tube or by using clothespins as clamps. Stick one end of the tube into the jar on the table and place the other in the jar on the chair. Remove the clothespins, or open the tube ends. Notice what happens.

When the water stops flowing, reverse the position of the jars. Then try both jars on the table.

You will see that: The water will flow as long as the level of water in one jar is lower than the level of water in the other jar.

Explanation: Gravity—the pull to the center of the earth—causes water to flow from the hose and reduces the pressure within it (at B). The air pressure is greater at A and water is forced into the hose.

A siphon, then, is a tube which uses air pressure and gravity to run water up over a high place.

Try to use the siphon without filling the hose with water. Does it work?

HOW TO COMPRESS AIR

Hold a glass with its mouth down and push it into a deep bowl of water.

You will see that: The water enters the glass a little way. No bubbles of air escape.

Explanation: The water forces the air into a smaller space. The small particles of air—the air molecules—are forced closer together, or compressed. Releasing compressed air furnishes power, and many machines work on this principle.

AIR CAN HOLD A STICK DOWN

Place a stick about the size of a yardstick on the table so that about a foot extends beyond the edge. Strike down on the free end. Notice that the other end of the stick pops up into the air.

Then lay a sheet or two of newspaper over the section of the stick that rests on the table. Smooth down the newspaper carefully by stroking from the center of the paper to the edges.

Hit the uncovered end of the stick a sharp glancing blow with a hammer.

You will see that: The covered stick won't move up. If you hit the end of the stick hard, it will break.

Explanation: When you smooth down the newspaper, you press all the air out from *under* the paper. The portion of the stick covered by the newspaper is held down by the air pressing down from above.

AIR SLOWS THINGS DOWN

Take two pieces of ordinary paper—newspaper will do. Crumple one into a ball. Lift your arms high and drop both pieces of paper at the same time.

You will see that: The crumpled paper drops right to the ground. The flat sheet floats slowly down.

Explanation: Air resists the movement of objects. The larger the surface pressed on by the air, the harder it is for the object to move through the air. The flat, wing-like sheet of paper has a larger surface than the crumpled ball.

Cars, trains and planes are streamlined to reduce the amount of surface to be moved through air, and thus to lessen air resistance.

SOME SURPRISES ABOUT AIR PRESSURE

1. Place two books 4 or 5 inches apart, and lay a sheet of paper over the books to cover the space between them. Blow through the space under the paper.

You will see that: The paper *sinks* between the books.

2. Hang two balloons a few inches apart and blow between them.

You will see that: The balloons move together.

Explanation: By causing air to move, you lessen the air pressure. The faster air moves, the less pressure it has. Airplanes can rise from the ground because of this.

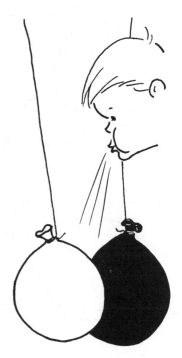

16

A PAPER HELICOPTER

Cut a sheet of paper so that you have a strip about 2 inches wide and 6 or 7 inches long. Hold the paper lengthwise and fold 10 to 12 narrow (¼-inch) strips on one end so that this end of the paper is weighted. (See illustration.) Then, starting from the other end, cut the paper in half lengthwise for a distance of 3 inches. Fold one half forward and the other back to make flaps.

Raise the helicopter above your head and holding it by one of the flaps, let go.

You will see that: The helicopter will whirl around until it reaches the ground almost directly beneath the spot from which it was dropped.

Explanation: Air flowing past the blades causes them to whirl. If the motor of a helicopter in flight failed, this is the way the whirling blades would break its fall.

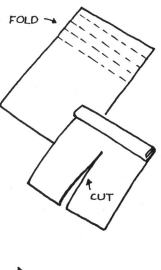

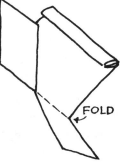

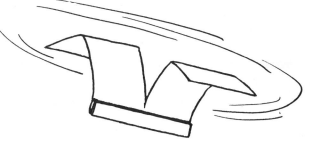

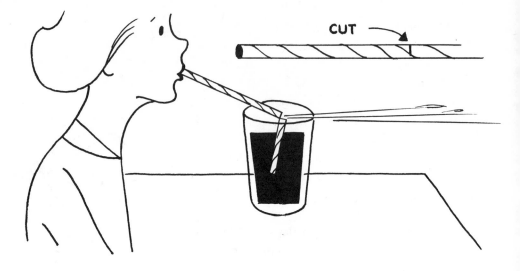

MAKE AN ATOMIZER

Make a slit in a paper straw about ⅓ from one end. Bend the straw at the slit and place the short section into a glass of water. Make sure the slit is no more than ¼ of an inch above the surface of the water. Blow hard through the far end of the long section of the straw.

You will see that: Water will enter the straw from the glass and possibly come out through the slit as a spray.

Explanation: The stream of air blowing over the top of the short section of straw reduces the pressure at that point. Normal pressure underneath forces the water up in the straw. The moving air blows the water off in drops.

Now you know how perfume atomizers, window-cleaning sprays, and other such devices work.

2. MATTER: WATER

FOOD IS MOSTLY WATER

Grate a potato or apple, or squeeze an orange or a piece of raw meat. Let a lettuce leaf stand in the air.

You will see that: Water (juice) will be pressed or squeezed out. The lettuce will wilt and grow smaller as the water in it dries up.

Explanation: Most of our foods contain large quantities of water. Potatoes are ¾ water. Green vegetables, such as lettuce, are 95% water. Beef is more than ⅗ water. Men and animals are made up of 60% to 70% water. Water is necessary to sustain life.

Do you know now why dehydrated foods—foods with the water removed—are used when it is necessary to save space?

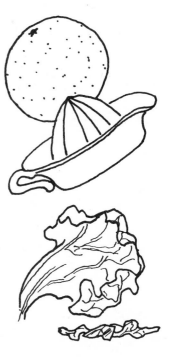

WATER COMING OUT OF THE AIR

ICE CUBES

FOOD DYE

Remove the label from an empty tin can. Fill it with ice and add water and a few drops of vegetable dye. Let it stand on the table for a short while.

You will see that: The can seems to be "sweating," for drops of water form on the outside.

Explanation: The drops are not colored and so they could not come from ice water leaking out of the can. The water comes from the air. Water vapor (water in the form of gas) in the air around the can has been cooled by the ice. The small particles of air, the air molecules, are slowed down when they become cold, so they move closer together (see chapter on heat) and change into liquid form. This is known as condensation.

Clouds are formed when large numbers of these drops of water collect on dust particles as the air is cooled. The drops fall to earth, as rain or snow, when they become too heavy to be held up by the pressure of air.

WATER GOING INTO THE AIR

1. Place an equal amount of water in two jars. Cap one of them. Place both on the table overnight.

You will see that: There is less water in the open jar than in the capped jar.

Explanation: Even at room temperature, the tiny particles or molecules of water move fast enough to fly out and escape into the air. When the jar is uncapped, this is exactly what happens. Some of the water turns into an invisible gas and escapes into the air. This process is known as evaporation.

Do you understand now how puddles disappear after the rain stops?

2. Place an equal amount of water in a large flat dish and in a deep narrow jar. Place both, uncovered, on the table to stand.

You will see that: There is less water in the flat dish than in the narrow jar.

Explanation: The molecules of water escape only from the surface. Therefore water evaporates faster from a large surface than from a small one.

Now you know why a large shallow puddle dries more quickly than a deep narrow one.

3. Hang two wet handkerchiefs to dry. Fan one with a cardboard, but let the other dry without fanning.

You will see that: The handkerchief that is fanned dries first.

Explanation: By replacing the moist air near the handkerchief with drier air, fanning speeds up evaporation. This is one of the reasons a windy day is a good day for drying clothes.

4. Half fill two dishes with water. Place one in the sun or on the radiator, and the other in the shade or another cool place.

You will see that: The dish in the sun loses its water first.

Explanation: The warmer the water, the greater is the speed of the molecules. The molecules move off into the air faster and speed up the rate of evaporation.

When evaporation takes place very quickly, it is known as boiling. (For more about evaporation and heat, see page 58.)

THE STRANGE STORY OF WATER'S SIZE

1. WATER EXPANDS WHEN HEATED

Fill a jar with water to the brim. Heat it gently in a saucepan containing an inch or two of boiling water.

You will see that: The water overflows.

Explanation: Water, like other liquids, fills more space when heated. The molecules bounce against one another more rapidly and spread out.

2. WATER CONTRACTS WHEN COOLED TO 39° FAHRENHEIT

Fill a jar (to the brim) and cool it in the refrigerator.

You will see that: The jar is not quite full.

Explanation: Until it goes down to 39° Fahrenheit, water contracts—takes up less space—as it gets colder. The molecules move more slowly, and closer together.

3. BUT WATER EXPANDS ON FREEZING

Fill a jar full of water and cap it with a piece of cardboard. Place it in the freezer of your refrigerator until it freezes.

You will see that: The cardboard cap is forced off.

Explanation: When water goes below 39° to its freezing temperature of 32°, it expands—takes up more room. It is one of the few things to behave this way.

If you use a tight cap on the jar as you freeze it, you will break the jar. Have you ever heard of water pipes bursting because water froze inside?

4. ICE IS LIGHTER THAN WATER

Place an ice cube or two in a glass of water.

You will see that: The ice cubes float.

Explanation: Because water expands as it freezes, ice is actually lighter than water. It is only 10/11ths as heavy.

This lucky fact speeds up the melting of ice in the warm sun. The layer of ice on the surface also slows down the freezing of the rest of the water in the lake and pond and protects the fish and other life there.

WATER ISN'T PURE

Place 5 tablespoons of tap water in a small glass dish and allow to stand.

You will see that: A white ring is left after the water evaporates.

Explanation: The white ring is formed by minerals which have dissolved in the water as it flowed through the soil.

Look at the inside of an old teakettle. Do you see the mineral deposit? That ring around your bathtub is not so much a ring of dirt as a ring of minerals from the water itself.

Try evaporating rain water. Does it contain minerals?

WHAT IS HARD WATER?

Make a powder out of a piece of chalk by grinding it with a stone. Add the powdered chalk to a jar full of water. Stir the mixture and filter it by pouring it through a handkerchief used as a strainer. Pour half of the mixture into another jar and add 1 tablespoon of washing soda or borax.

Add the same amount of soap powder to both jars. Shake them.

You will see that: The water to which you added washing soda produces more suds.

Explanation: You made hard water by adding chalk (or limestone) and then softened part of it with the washing soda. Certain materials such as limestone (the chalk) make water "hard." Hard water does not mix well with soap. The washing soda added to one jar softened the water so that it mixed more easily with soap than the hard water.

The name "hard water" is said to have been given during the Civil War. When soldiers found their beans were hard after being cooked in a particular water, they left behind signs, "Hard Water."

Do you have hard water? You can test your tap water by comparing the amount of suds it produces with that made in the hard and soft waters of this experiment.

WHAT HAPPENS WHEN SOMETHING DISSOLVES?

Fill a glass with water to the brim. Slowly shake in salt, stirring carefully with a thin wire or a toothpick. See how much salt you can add without making the water overflow.

You will see that: If you are careful, you can add an entire shaker of salt to the full glass without spilling any water.

Explanation: You are making a solution of water and salt. It is believed that as the salt dissolves, molecules of salt separate and fill the spaces between the molecules of water.

INVISIBLE INK

To a tablespoon or two of salt, gradually add a similar amount of hot water.

Then, dip a clean pen or a small stick (the clean end of a used match is fine) into the solution. Write your message on a sheet of paper.

At first, your message can be seen. Let the paper stand for ½ hour or so and the writing disappears.

Rub over the sheet of paper with the side of a soft pencil.

You will see that: Your message will be clearly visible.

Explanation: The water evaporates from your solution, leaving the small particles of salt clinging to the paper. These make the paper rough and uneven, but they are too small to be seen. When you rub over the paper, the pencil lead darkens them and causes the particles of salt to stand out.

MAKING A CRYSTAL

Gradually stir ¼ cup of sugar into hot water until the water is too full to accept any more. Then hang a string in the solution and let it stand for several days or a week.

You will see that: A crystal forms on the string.

Explanation: The water evaporates in the air, leaving behind the sugar, in the form of a solid crystal.

WATER PRESSURE

Punch 3 or 4 small holes, one above the other, along the side of an empty milk carton or a large can. Cover the holes with a long strip of adhesive tape and fill the carton with water. Then place the can in the sink or a basin and pull off the tape.

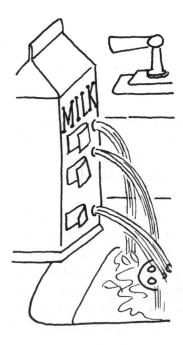

You will see that: The stream from the lowest hole travels farthest.

Explanation: The water at the bottom of the carton has the force exerted by the pressure of the water above it.

Like air, water has pressure.

Water pressure depends, as your experiment shows, on the water's depth. Many cities pump water into raised tanks. This is done to give the water enough force to run up into people's homes from pipes beneath the ground.

WHICH WAY DOES WATER RUN?

Remove the cover of a quart-size can. With a nail, punch holes around the can about 2 inches from the bottom. Cover the holes with a circle of adhesive tape.

Fill the can with water. Center it on a sheet of newspaper in a sink or basin and strip off the tape.

You will see that: The water travels the same distance from each of the holes. Your streams of water make a circle on the newspaper.

Explanation: Pressure is the same at the same depth. Water pressure is the same in all directions if the depth is the same.

PRESSURE AND SHAPE AND SIZE

Punch a hole 1 inch from the bottom of an empty, frozen orange juice can and do the same to a much taller can. Cover each hole with a strip of tape.

Fill both cans with water to the same level. Of course, it will take more water to bring the larger can to the same depth.

Place the cans in a sink or basin and pull off the strips of tape.

You will see that: The streams of water shoot out to the same distance.

Explanation: Hard as it is to believe, the pressure of the water does not depend on the size or shape of its container but on the *depth* of the water.

WATER SEEKS ITS OWN LEVEL

Insert a funnel into one end of a 2- or 3-foot strip of rubber tubing or a narrow hose. Into the other end of the tubing, insert a glass straw or tube.

Holding both the funnel and the glass tubing upright, as in the illustration, pour water into the funnel.

You will see that: The level of the water in the funnel and in the glass tube will be the same.

Explanation: The same pressure pushes on both and so the depth of the water is the same.

Try raising and lowering the funnel a little and notice what happens.

28

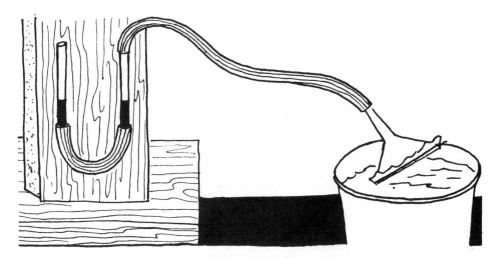

MEASURING WATER PRESSURE

Connect two glass or clear plastic straws with a short length of rubber tubing. Attach the straws to a support, as in the illustration. Use adhesive tape to bind them to the block of wood.

Color some water with vegetable dye and pour it into the tubes until the straws have water to their halfway mark.

Cover a funnel with a circle of thin rubber (from a balloon or old rubber sheet). Stretch the rubber taut and tie it tightly with thread or a rubber band. Attach the funnel to one of the straws with a long length of rubber tubing.

With this gauge, or manometer, you can now measure water pressure.

Fill a pail with water and test the device. Put the funnel into the pail of water—first just below the surface, then halfway down, then all the way under.

You will see that: The colored water moves lower in the closed straw and higher in the open one, as the funnel goes deeper into the pail.

Explanation: The pressure of the water on the rubber of the funnel forces the movement of the colored water.

With your manometer, compare pressure near the surface and toward the bottom of the water. Compare the pressure of the same depth of water in a milk carton and a frozen-juice can. Compare the pressure of the same depth of water and other liquids about the house—orange juice, rubbing alcohol, oil, milk.

A HOT WATER BAG LIFTS BOOKS

Fit a hot water bag with a 1-hole rubber stopper or cork. Punch a hole in the bottom of an open can or carton and fit the hole with another 1-hole stopper or cork. Place short glass or plastic straws into each of the stoppers. You will also need 4 to 5 feet of rubber tubing to connect the hot water bag to the can.

Fill the hot water bag with water and stopper it. Fit on the rubber tubing, attaching the other end to the glass tube of the can. Rest the bag on the floor and press it gently until water fills the tube. Then fill the can with water.

Put a large, flat board on the hot water bag and then stack books or blocks on top of it. Raise the can up.

You will see that: As you raise the water, the books move.

Explanation: The pressure increases at the bottom of the tube as you increase the height of the tube. Increased pressure on one part of the enclosed water is carried by the water in all directions equally.

This is how the hydraulic press works. A barber chair is raised by a hydraulic press that uses oil as its liquid, and the hydraulic brake in the automobile uses oil and alcohol.

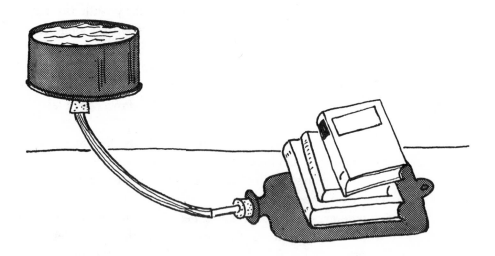

YOU "WEIGH" LESS IN WATER

Attach a spring or a rubber band to a nail on a board.

Fill a small bottle or screw-top can with water. Put a string around the bottle and attach it to the rubber band. Note how much the rubber band stretches. Then lower the bottle into a pail of water and notice what happens to the rubber band.

You will see that: The rubber band is stretched less.

Explanation: The bottle appears to weigh less because the water exerts a lifting force, known as buoyancy. An object in water is buoyed up by a force equal to the weight of the water it displaces.

WHAT FLOATS?

Put an empty stoppered medicine bottle in a pan of water. Observe what happens. Half fill the bottle in a pan of water, stopper it, and place it in the pan again. Fill it completely and watch again.

You will see that: The empty bottle floats but as you fill it with water it sinks lower and lower. The full bottle sinks.

Explanation: Objects float in water if they are lighter than a quantity of water that would take up an equal amount of space. The bottle continues to take up the same amount of space as it gets heavier. When it is heavier than the water which would occupy an equal amount of space, it sinks. Place wooden, plastic and brass buttons in a glass of water. Which float?

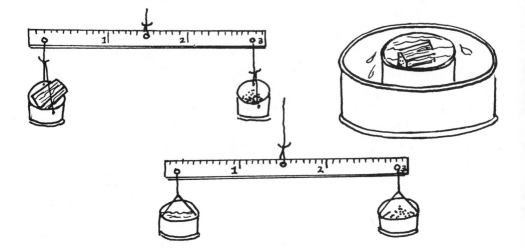

A FLOATING OBJECT DISPLACES OWN WEIGHT

Weigh a small block of wood in a large dry can. You can use the yard-stick balance described on page 7.

Then take out the wood and place a smaller can into the larger one. Fill the small can to the brim with water. Carefully push the wood block into the water until no more flows over into the larger can. Remove the small can carefully.

Weigh the large can with its overflowed water on the yardstick balance.

You will see that: The weight of the water in the large can equals the weight of the wood in the large can.

Explanation: An object that floats displaces its own weight of water. A boat floats because it displaces water that weighs as much as it does.

BOTTLE SUBMARINE

Half fill a small medicine bottle or tiny glass with water.

Then pour water into a tall jar or glass. Hold the water in the small bottle with your finger and put the bottle, upside down, into the tall glass.

If the bottle floats on top of the water, add water to the bottle. If it sinks, pour out a little.

When the bottle is just barely floating, fill the tall jar with water to its top. Cover the jar with a circle of balloon rubber. Stretch it taut, and tie it tightly.

Hold the palm of your hand over the rubber and push downwards. Then release your hand.

You will see that: The bottle dives down. When you remove your hand, the bottle floats again.

Explanation: When you press with your hand, you force the air inside the bottle to compress—to occupy less space—since water cannot be compressed. This leaves room for more water. When the added water enters the bottle, the bottle becomes heavier than the water which it displaces and sinks.

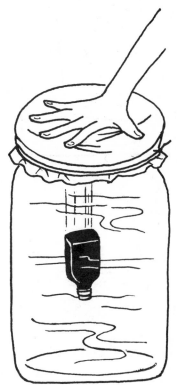

FLOAT AN EGG

Place an egg in a glass of fresh water. Notice what happens. Add salt to the water, stir gently, and observe what happens.

Put a tack in the eraser end of a pencil and place the pencil in a glass of fresh water. Add salt, stir gently, and notice what happens.

You will see that: In the fresh water the egg and the pencil sink. As you add salt, they float higher and higher.

Explanation: A denser liquid has a greater upward lift or buoyancy. Salt makes water denser. Now you know why ships ride higher in ocean water than in fresh water, and why you find it easier to swim in the ocean than in a lake.

SURFACE TENSION

1. Using a cardboard or a fork as a carrier, place a needle on the surface of water in a dish. Carefully remove the carrier.

You will see that: The needle will float.

Explanation: The needle is heavier than the amount of water it displaces and should be expected to sink. It floats, however, because of an invisible elastic skin. When water comes in contact with air, the molecules on the surface of the water huddle closer together and form a thin film or skin over the surface.

2. Dip a piece of soap in your dish with the floating needle.

You will see that: The needle sinks immediately.

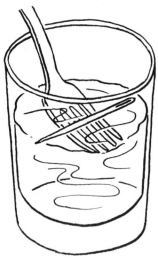

Explanation: The soap reduces the surface tension.

It is one of the reasons we use soap for cleaning. By lowering surface tension, soap makes water able to wet greasy surfaces.

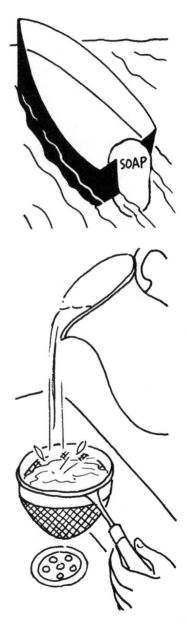

SOAP BOAT

Use a piece of soap as the fuel for a cardboard boat. Place a notch in your boat and insert a dab of soap. Put your boat in a tub or basin of water.

The boat will sail until the soap reduces the surface tension of all the water in your lake.

HOLDING WATER IN A STRAINER

Pour some liquid oil over a small strainer (a tea strainer will do). The oil coats the sharp edges of the wire. Shake the strainer so that the holes are open. Hold the strainer over a sink or basin. Carefully pour water into the strainer from a glass or pitcher, letting it run down the inside of the strainer.

You will see that: The strainer fills. The water pushes through the openings but cannot get through.

Explanation: Surface tension—the invisible elastic skin—keeps the water from running through. Touch the bottom of the strainer with your finger and the water will run through because your finger breaks the surface of the water.

HOW MANY DIMES WILL IT HOLD?

Place a jar or a glass in a basin. Fill the jar to the brim with water. Drop in dimes or thin metal washers, holding them by their edges.

You will see that: You can drop a surprising number of coins into the jar before the water flows over.

Explanation: Surface tension permits you to heap the water quite high before it breaks and the water runs over.

3. MECHANICAL ENERGY AND MACHINES

Watch a ball bouncing, a train rushing by, the sun going through the sky. See an automobile wheel turn, an airplane fly, a screw boring into a piece of wood.

All of these are examples of motion.

The science that describes and explains these motions is called mechanics.

WHY DO THINGS FALL DOWN?

Suspend various things from strings—a marble, a can, a fork, a toy. Hold each up or tie it to a rod. Cut each string.

You will see that: The objects all fall.

Explanation: The force of gravity pulls objects down toward the center of the earth.

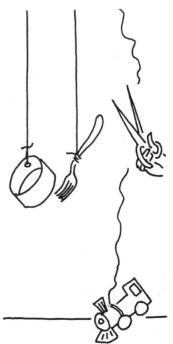

This pull of gravity sometimes helps us and sometimes works against us. Gravity keeps us and everything around us from flying off into space, but it makes it harder for us to send a rocket to the moon. Compare how much easier it is to walk *down* a flight of stairs than it is to walk *up* a flight. When we climb and when we lift something we need to make the upward pull or push greater than the downward pull of the earth.

WHICH FALLS FASTER?

Stand on a sturdy table or on a high chair and drop two objects at the same time—a heavy object and a light one.

You will see that: Both reach the ground at the same time.

Explanation: The weight of an object does not affect its speed as it falls.

But we know that a feather doesn't fall as fast as a stone and that a man with a parachute falls more slowly than a man without one. The shape of the feather and the parachute are important because they offer a larger surface to the air and are slowed down by the air's resistance.

HOW DO YOU PITCH A BALL?

Throw a ball straight out as far as you can. Notice where it falls. Now with just as much energy, throw the ball slightly up and as far as you can.

You will see that: The ball thrown slightly upward lands farther away.

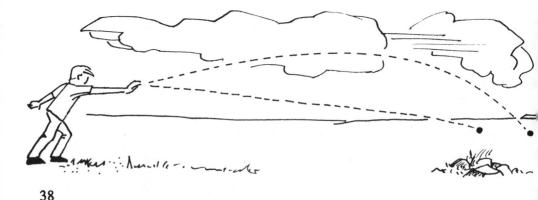

Explanation: The ball thrown upward has farther to fall before it hits the ground. Meanwhile it is also going away from the thrower. Therefore it has more time to go a greater distance before it strikes the ground.

If two balls are thrown straight by boys of the same height, the balls will strike the ground at the same time. This is true even if one boy uses more energy. His ball will go farther but will strike the ground at the same time. The pull of the earth's gravity is the same for both, but the greater energy applied causes one ball to travel farther out, in the same time, before falling.

FALLING WEIGHT DOES WORK

Lift a little pebble and a large stone from the floor and place each on a table. Lay a flat tin can on the floor near the table. Push off the pebble so that it strikes the can. What happens? Push off the large stone so that it strikes the can. What happens?

You will see that: The large stone makes a large dent in the can while the pebble barely scratches it.

Explanation: The large stone stores up more energy. It took more energy to lift it than it did to lift the little stone. Objects which require more energy to lift have more energy when they fall.

Have you ever seen a pile driver work?

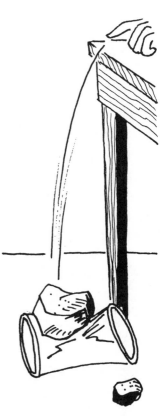

SPRINKLERS AND ROCKETS

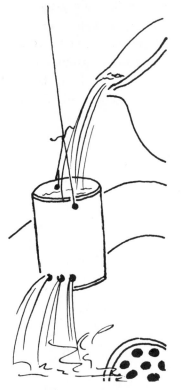

With a hammer and small nail, make 4 small holes near the bottom of an empty can. The holes should be in a straight line about ¼ inch apart.

Run wire around the rim of the top of the can, or punch 2 more holes near the top through which to thread the wire. Hang the wire from a piece of string, and then tie the string to a hanger and support it on a ledge or rod (or in one hand) over a sink or basin.

Pour water into the can. What happens?

You will see that: The water goes out the holes in one direction—and the can swings in the opposite direction.

Explanation: For every action, there is an equal opposite reaction. As the water rushes out forward it causes the can to move backward. Revolving lawn sprinklers work in much the same way.

When you row a boat, the oars push the water backward and the boat moves forward.

Blow up a balloon and then let go of it. When the air escapes from the balloon, the balloon moves in the opposite direction from the escaping air.

This is the law of motion that makes both rockets and jet planes work. As hot gases are forced out the back, the jet or rocket shoots forward at high speed.

CENTER OF GRAVITY

Roll a ball on a level surface. Do it several times and notice what happens. Now stick some clay on the ball at one point. Roll the ball again. What happens? Repeat it a few times.

You will see that: At first the ball keeps on rolling and stops in any position. When the clay is fixed to one point, the ball always stops rolling with the clay touching the surface on which the ball is rolled.

Explanation: An object acts as though all of its weight is concentrated at one point. This is known as its center of gravity. It is likely to be located at the part where most of the weight is. An object will tend to move until its center of gravity is at its lowest possible point.

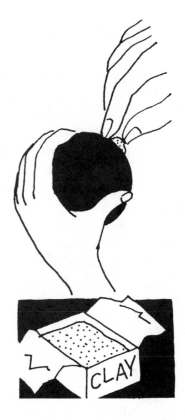

The center of gravity of the ball is at its very center. It is balanced at any point since rolling neither raises nor lowers its center of gravity. When we put on the clay, however, the center of gravity is changed and the ball will tend to roll until the clay is at its lowest possible point.

STOP AND GO

Fill a toy wagon with blocks, or pile blocks on a skate. Start it slowly, pull it for a time, then slowly stop it.

Then start the wagon quickly, pull it for a time, and stop it quickly.

You will see that: It is harder to start the wagon than to keep it moving. The quicker you want to start it, the harder you need to pull. The faster it is moving, the more energy you need to stop it. Also, the more quickly you want to stop it, the more force you need.

Explanation: It takes more force (push or pull) to start and to stop an object than to keep it moving. Objects that are moving tend to keep moving, and objects at rest tend to remain at rest. This is known as inertia.

Draw a line on the floor and try to run to it and stop. You will find that you may be able to stop your feet but your upper body will continue to move forward.

Now you know why you lurch forward when a car stops suddenly.

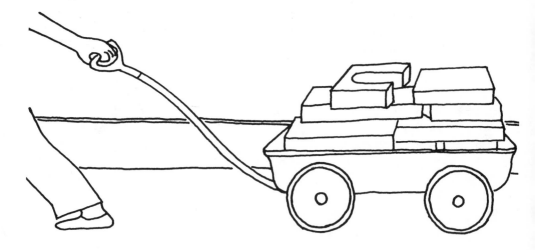

MORE ABOUT INERTIA

Place a book on a sheet of paper. Then jerk the paper suddenly.

You will see that: The book doesn't move.

Explanation: When you pull the paper quickly, it is easier to move the paper from under the book than to move the book. Inertia—the tendency of objects at rest to stay motionless—is responsible.

WHY USE WHEELS?

Borrow an oil drum or small barrel for this experiment. Place the barrel in an upright position and push it across the room. Then turn it on its side and roll it back.

You will see that: It is much easier to roll, than to push the can.

Explanation: There is less rolling friction than sliding friction. In sliding, the bumps on the rough surfaces catch against each other. In rolling, the bumps of the wheel roll over the bumps of the rough surface without rubbing as much.

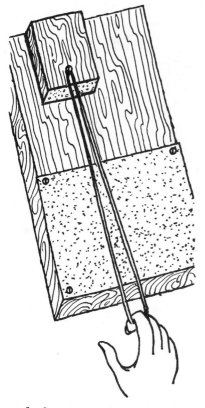

WHAT IS FRICTION?

Tack a piece of sandpaper to half of a board. Then place a tack in a small but heavy block or other piece of finished wood. The tack should be free enough so that you can loop on a thin rubber band.

Holding the block by the rubber band, pull it across the smooth half of the board. Notice how much the rubber band is stretched. Then pull the block across the sandpaper. Again, watch the rubber band.

You will see that: The rubber band stretches more when you pull your block across the rough sandpaper. The greater stretch of the rubber band indicates you are using more effort.

Explanation: When two things move in contact with one another, they resist moving. No two surfaces are completely smooth —look at something you think is smooth under a magnifying glass. Therefore, the bumps of one surface catch against the bumps in the other. The resistance that results when the surfaces rub against each other is known as friction.

The amount of friction depends on the kinds of surfaces in contact with one another and the force pressing them together. The rougher the surfaces, the greater will be the friction. The greater the weight of the objects, the greater will be the friction.

Some friction is necessary. New tires with deep, sharp treads are safer than worn-out "smooth" tires. The greater friction between the new tires and the road prevents skidding and spinning.

But too much friction wastes energy, produces unwanted heat, and wears away parts.

WHY DO WE OIL MACHINES?

Slide two blocks of wood over each other. Then rub soap or petroleum jelly over each surface, and slide the blocks over each other again.

You will see that: The surfaces slide more easily after the soap is put on.

Explanation: The soap fills in the low places of the surfaces of the wood and also forms a coat over the surfaces. The woods, therefore, do not touch one another and cannot rub. Instead, the soapy surfaces slide against one another with less friction. Try coating a dull safety pin with soap. Notice how much more easily you can use it.

Water, too, can act as a lubricant to smooth a surface. Coal chutes are sprinkled with water to make the chutes smoother. In ice skating, a little of the ice melts under the skate and the skater is thus able to slide over a film of water.

For most tools and machines, we use oil or grease to do the job the soap did on our blocks of wood. The oil and grease smooth the surfaces so that there will be less rubbing. They are used because they do not dry up as quickly as soap or water or other lubricants.

Do you know now why a drop or two of oil will stop the squeak in a door hinge? It's handy to know, too, that a little wax (a kind of hard oil) will help you open and close your desk drawers more easily.

MACHINES

A machine is anything which makes work easier because it helps us in some way to push or pull. The machine may allow less effort on our part, or it may increase speed, increase distance, or change direction.

All of our complicated machines are based on two or more simple machines which have existed for thousands of years. These are the lever, the wheel and axle, the pulley, the inclined plane, the wedge, and the screw.

SEESAWS AND SCALES ARE LEVERS

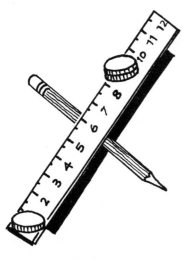

Place a pencil under the 6-inch mark of a 1-foot ruler. Balance the ruler.

Then place a penny on each end of the ruler and notice what happens. Cover the coin on the 12-inch mark with another penny. What happens?

Move the two-coin weight closer and closer to the pencil. What happens?

You will see that: The two coins (twice as heavy as the one coin) balance the one coin when they rest on the 9-inch mark of the ruler. When you move the coins even closer to the pencil, one coin is able to lift two coins.

Explanation: This is exactly what happens on a seesaw. You can seesaw with a person heavier than you if he is moved in close enough to the center.

Instead of placing a pencil under a ruler, as you did in the experiment above, suspend the ruler on a string and balance the coins.

Both scale and seesaw are <u>levers</u>. A lever is merely a stiff bar able to turn about one point, known as the fulcrum. In the seesaw experiment, the ruler acts as the bar, the pencil as the fulcrum. Many levers have fulcrums at an end of the stiff bar, instead of in the center.

You may be familiar with such levers as the crowbar, the shovel, the baseball bat, but you may not know that pliers, scissors, tin shears and nut crackers are pairs of levers. Our fingers, arms and legs are levers. So are knives, forks,. rakes and brooms. How many more levers can you think of?

WHEEL AND AXLE

Take off the cover of a pencil sharpener. Tie a length of string around the axle of the sharpener, as in the illustration. Attach several books to the free end of the string. Turn the handle of the sharpener until the books are raised to the desk or table on which the sharpener is mounted. Untie the books and lift them the same distance by hand.

You will see that: You use less effort lifting the books when they are attached to the sharpener.

Explanation: You are using the sharpener as a wheel and axle (wheel and rod) to lessen the force needed to lift the weight. This is really a lever that spins in a circle.

Other examples of a wheel and axle are a doorknob, a key and a windlass.

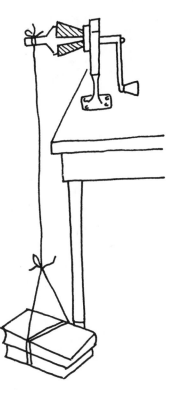

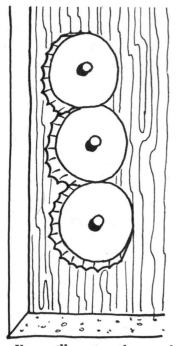

BOTTLE-TOP GEARS

Collect three bottle caps. Be sure they are not bent. Punch a hole through the center of each with a nail. Place them on a block of wood close enough to one another so that they touch. Tack the caps down loosely with thin nails so that they turn easily.

Turn one of the caps with your finger or with a pencil and notice what happens to the others.

You will see that: When you turn one cap, all three turn.

Explanation: The ridges of each cap act like the teeth of a gear and interlock or mesh with the teeth of the gear next to it.

You will notice that each gear turns in the opposite direction to the gear next to it. When the gear in the middle turns counterclockwise, the two on the ends turn clockwise, for example. Thus gears can be used to change the direction of the turning of an axle. A good example of this is when a car is shifted into reverse to make the rear wheels turn backward.

In addition to changing direction, gears also are used to change force or speed. Speed is increased when a small gear is turned by a large one, and force is increased when a large gear is turned by a small one.

The teeth on the rim of the gears are to prevent slipping. You can see then that gears are a form of the wheel and axle.

Examine the gears of an egg beater and of an old clock. Also, notice the chains that connect a bicycle's gears.

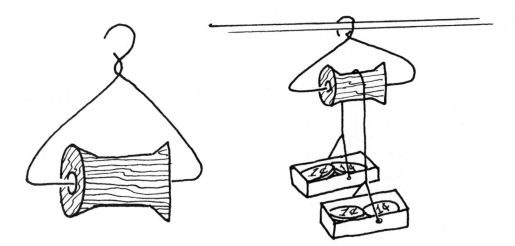

HOW A PULLEY WORKS

Thread a stiff wire through a spool and shape the ends into a hook, as in the illustration. You can use a metal clothes hanger, bending the wire back and forth until it breaks.

Suspend the spool (pulley) from a rod or hook. Place a piece of string several feet long over the spool and attach a small paper box to each end. Place several coins in one of the boxes. Then add various coins and find out what weight you need to lift the other box.

When the two sides are balanced, pull down one box 2 inches. What happens to the other box?

You will see that: Equal weights are needed to balance the boxes. When you pull one box down 2 inches, the other box moves 2 inches up.

Explanation: You are using your spool and string as a single fixed *pulley*. It gives no increase of force but simply changes direction. In this case it also allows you to pull down in order to lift up.

Pulleys help us to raise windows, get the flag to the top of the pole, move clotheslines. Nearly all cranes, hoists, and elevators make use of one or more pulleys.

BLOCK AND TACKLE

This is an experiment for you and your parents or two friends.

Give a length of broomstick or doweling to each of the grownups and ask them to stand a few feet apart. Then tie down one end of a length of clothesline or strong rope to one of the sticks and weave the rope in and out around the sticks, as in the illustration.

You pull on the free end of the rope.

You will see that: You will be able to pull the two sticks together although strong adults try to keep them apart.

Explanation: You have formed a combination of pulleys. The force you apply is increased by the number of ropes holding the weight. In this experiment, you increase your force each time you wrap the rope around the broomstick. A small force moving a long distance results in a greater force moving a shorter distance.

A group of pulleys, called a block and tackle, is used for loading ships lifting shovels of cranes, tightening fences on a farm, lowering and lifting lifeboats, pianos, safes, machinery.

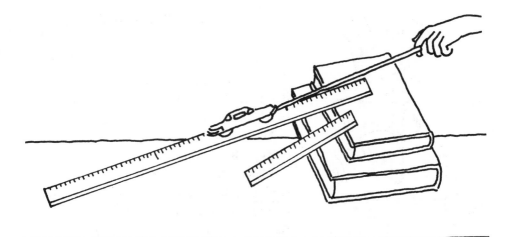

SOMETHING ABOUT RAMPS

Prop rulers of different lengths on a pile of books. Attach a thin rubber band to a small toy automobile or tack the rubber band to a block. Pull the object up the different ramps and notice how far the rubber band is stretched in each case. Then pull the toy straight up to the books without using a ramp. Notice how far the rubber band is stretched.

You will see that: The longer the ruler, the less the rubber band is stretched. The band is stretched most when the object is pulled straight up into the air to the height of the books.

Explanation: The ramp or inclined plane is a machine that makes it possible to climb gradually. The object rises more slowly but with less effort. When you lift the object straight up, it takes more force over a shorter distance, but you do the same amount of work. When going up the ramps, less force is used but the distance travelled is longer. The longer the ramp, the less force used. But the object must travel farther to reach the same height.

Gangplanks, winding roads up a mountain, even stairs are all examples of inclined planes. Watch the next time a truckman has to raise a heavy load from the ground to the truck. See whether he uses a ramp to make his job easier.

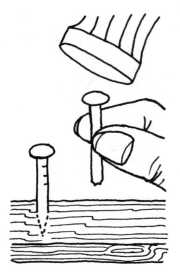

NAILS AND KNIVES

Hammer a nail into a block of wood. Pull it out with the claw of the hammer. Then blunt the end of the nail by filing it down. Try to hammer it into the same block of wood.

You will see that: You have more difficulty hammering the filed nail in.

Explanation: The end of the nail is a <u>wedge</u> until you file it down. A wedge is two ramps or inclined planes back to back. As the nail is forced into the block, its sloping surfaces make the job a more gradual one. You need not bang as hard to get the nail in.

Knives, axes, stakes, needles, pins, chisels are among the common wedges.

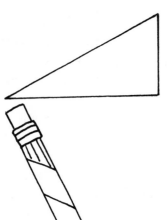

SCREWS AND SCREW TOPS

Cut out a triangle (or ramp) from a sheet of paper, as shown in the illustration. Roll the ramp around a pencil. What do you have?

You will see that: You have made a screw.

Explanation: A <u>screw</u> is really a ramp or inclined plane wrapped around a round form. You know about screws that hold together pieces of wood or metal. Now examine the jars in the house. Do some of the covers screw on?

Do you know that a piano stool is lifted by a screw? Other examples of the screw are a food chopper, electric fan, airplane propeller, skate clamp and vise.

4. HEAT

Heat isn't a thing. It doesn't occupy space. It has no weight. Like light, sound and electricity, heat is a form of energy. Heat does work. It is energy that raises the temperature of a thing by causing the molecules in that thing to move faster.

CAN YOU TELL HOT FROM COLD?

Prepare three bowls or pans. Half fill one with hot water—not hot enough to burn! Place lukewarm water in the second. Pour very cold water in the third. Set them in a row on the table, with the lukewarm water in the center.

Place your left hand in the hot water and your right hand in the cold water. Keep them in for a few minutes. Then take them out, shake off the water, and put both into the middle bowl. How do they feel?

You will see that: Your left hand feels cold and your right hand feels warm.

Explanation: When you put your hands in the center bowl, some heat from your left hand leaves and goes to warm up the water, and so you feel a loss of heat—your left hand feels cold. Heat from the water travels to your cold right hand, and so you feel a gain of heat—your right hand feels warm.

COLD   LUKEWARM   HOT

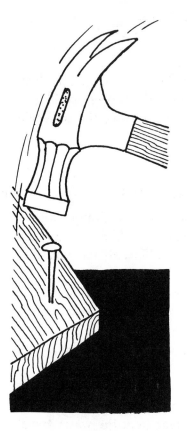

HOW TO MAKE HEAT BY FRICTION

1. Feel a nail and hammer. Then hammer the nail into a piece of wood. Feel both nail and hammer again.

You will see that: Both nail and hammer are warm.

Explanation: The energy of your muscle is given to the moving hammer, and goes from the hammer to the nail. Because of the added energy, the molecules of hammer and nail move faster and the heat is increased.

2. Put your hands on your cheeks to see how warm your hands are. Now rub your hands together quickly 10 times. Bring them to your cheeks.

You will see that: After rubbing, your hands are warmer than before.

Explanation: Friction (rubbing) causes movement of molecules. So the temperature of your hands was raised.

HOW TO MAKE HEAT BY RADIANT ENERGY

Pour a little cold water into a saucer. Place it on a window in the sunlight. Let it stand for a while, and then test it with your hand or a thermometer.

You will see that: The water gets warmer and warmer.

Explanation: The sun sends out rays of energy (infrared) which warm an object when they strike it. This is known as radiant energy.

HOW TO MAKE HEAT FROM ELECTRICITY

Feel an electric bulb (not fluorescent) which has not been used for a while. Then turn on the electricity and feel the bulb. (Don't wait too long.)

You will see that: The bulb feels warm.

Explanation: Part of the electrical energy is converted to heat as it passes through the wires (filament) in the bulb. Toasters, irons and heaters make use of the same principle. Electric currents can produce large quantities of heat as they go through a wire coil.

HOW HEAT BLOWS UP A BALLOON

Stretch a rubber balloon over the neck of an "empty" bottle. Put the bottle into hot water, or light a candle and hold the bottle over the flame.

You will see that: The balloon blows up.

Explanation: When heat is added, the molecules of air in the bottle move faster and farther apart and therefore the gas (air) occupies more space. As more and more air flows into the balloon from the bottle, the walls of the elastic balloon are pushed out by the air. Heat has caused the air to expand. What do you think will happen when you remove the heat? Try it. Now you know why it is necessary to check balloon tires during hot weather.

WHY SIDEWALKS HAVE SPACES

Hammer a nail into a tin can. Ease the nail out. Put it in again to make sure that the hole is large enough for the nail. Then, holding the nail with a pair of pliers, scissors or forceps, heat the nail over a candle, in hot water, or over the stove. Try to put it into the hole in the can.

You will see that: The heated nail does not fit into the hole in the can.

Explanation: Heat expands solids. The molecules in the solid move faster, spread apart and occupy more space.

Now you know why sidewalks are laid in sections with spaces between, and why a door is sometimes difficult to open and close during the summer.

HOW A THERMOMETER WORKS

Fit a medicine bottle or small jar with a cork and tube. You can use a glass straw or the medicine bottle tube. Fill the bottle to the brim with water colored with a drop or two of ink or vegetable dye, and cap it securely. Mark the line the water rises to in the tube.

Place your bottle in a pot of hot water or hold it over a burning candle. Notice what happens.

Cool the bottle and watch the results.

You will see that: The water rises into the tube when heated. It drops lower in the tube when cooled.

Explanation: Liquids expand when heated and contract when cooled. The mercury thermometer we use is based on these facts.

We do not measure temperature directly, but rather the changes it produces. The liquid of the thermometer (usually mercury) absorbs heat and expands when it comes in contact with anything warmer than itself. The liquid of the thermometer grows smaller (contracts) when in contact with something cooler than itself. Temperature is really a measure of whether one object will give heat to or absorb heat from another object.

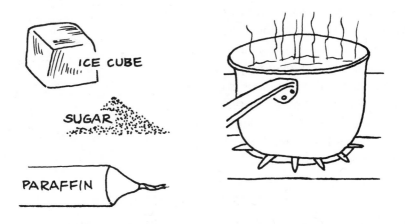

HOW HEAT CHANGES SOLID TO LIQUID

1. Put an ice cube into a tin can or a small pot and apply heat.
2. Heat sugar in a can or pot.
3. Put the paraffin of a candle in a can and apply heat.

You will see that: Solids turn to liquid when heated.

Explanation: As you add heat, you speed up the molecules of the substance so that the solid first expands and then changes to a liquid in which the molecules can move about more freely. We call this process melting.

Have you ever seen pictures of the pots of red-hot molten steel over a furnace? Afterward, the liquid steel is poured into molds and solidifies—becomes a solid—as it cools.

HOW HEAT CHANGES LIQUID TO GAS

Heat a little water in a pot or jar and keep heating it. Measure the temperature with a cooking thermometer from time to time.

You will see that: You get steam, the gaseous state of water, but the thermometer will not rise above 212° Fahrenheit.

Explanation: You speed up the molecules until they are flying about and form· a gas. The temperature rises to the boiling point of 212°, but not above 212°, allowing all the water to boil away.

Hold a cold glass over the pot while it is steaming but after the heat is turned off. You'll find that drops of water will form in the glass. Lessening the temperature to below 212° allows some of the gas to change back to liquid form.

HOW EVAPORATION COOLS

1. Put a tablespoonful of water in one dish, and a tablespoonful of rubbing alcohol in another dish. Which disappears—evaporates—first?

2. Wet one hand with water and the other with rubbing alcohol. Fan both in the air. Which hand feels cooler?

You will see that: Alcohol evaporates (turns into a vapor or gas) more quickly than water. Both alcohol and water cool, but alcohol cools more.

Explanation: Heat is absorbed from the surface of your skin as the water or alcohol evaporates. Therefore the temperature of your body is lowered. The more rapid evaporation of alcohol results in greater coolness.

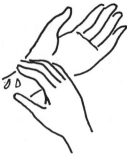

This is why an alcohol rub is given to someone with a high fever.

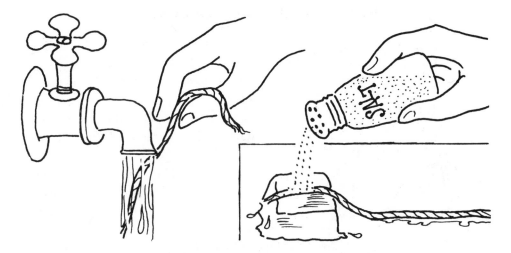

FUN WITH ICE AND SALT

By making use of what you've learned about the transfer of heat, you can perform scientific "magic."

Dip a string in water until it is thoroughly wet. Lay it across the top of an ice cube. Sprinkle a little salt along the line of the string.

You will see that: In a few minutes you can lift the cube by the string.

Explanation: Where the salt strikes the ice, it lowers the freezing point of ice (32° Fahrenheit) to a little below 32° and causes it to melt a little. As the ice refreezes, it encloses the string.

FUN WITH ICE CUBES

1. Squeeze two ice cubes together in a towel and hold them for several minutes.

You will see that: When you stop pressing, the two cubes are frozen together.

Explanation: The pressure causes the ice to melt by lowering its melting temperature. The two cubes freeze together when the pressure is released and the freezing point goes up.

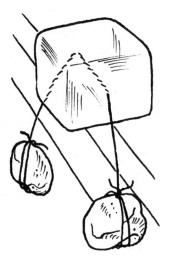

2. Tie stones or other weights to the ends of a thin wire. Hang the wire and weights over an ice cube or larger block of ice.

You will see that: The wire passes through the ice without breaking it, leaving a solid cube.

Explanation: The line of ice directly under the wire melts because the pressure lowers the melting point, but the water freezes again as the wire passes through. Does this explain how you skate over ice?

DEGREE AND CALORIE

1. Place a small pan of water and a large pot of water on high flames on two stove burners at the same time. At the point when each bubbles, put in a cooking thermometer and measure the temperature.

You will see that: The small panful begins to boil (or bubble) long before the large pan. Both, however, show a temperature of 212° Fahrenheit or 100° Centigrade at the boiling point.

Explanation: More heat is needed to boil the larger amount of water.

2. Place an open can of cold water in each pot. Watch their temperature to find out which can gets hotter.

You will see that: The large pan will raise the can of water to a higher temperature.

Explanation: Both pots of boiling water have a temperature of 212°. But the large pot can give off more heat energy than the small pot.

Total heat is measured by the calorie, the amount of heat needed to raise one gram of water one degree Centigrade. (The "Calorie" we mean when we talk about food is equal to 1,000 small calories.)

WHY NOT METAL HANDLES?

1. Put a silver spoon into a hot cup of chocolate. Feel the heat of the spoon after a few seconds.

2. Melt candle wax. Knead it into lumps as it cools and press it at various points onto a steel knitting needle. Dig the point of the needle into a cork and use that as a handle. Then hold the other end of the needle (not a plastic tip) over a burning candle or other source of heat.

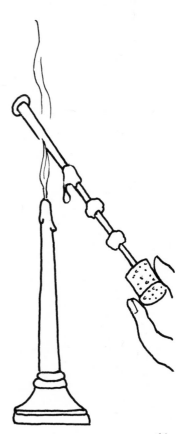

You will see that: The silver spoon gets hot. The needle gets hot enough to melt the wax.

Explanation: The molecules of the hot chocolate, moving very quickly, bump into the molecules of the spoon. These bump into the molecules next to them, which bump into the molecules next to them until the heat energy is exhausted. The same thing happens with the molecules of the needle and wax. Metals are good conductors of heat.

The molecules of the cork are not as easy to move as those of the metal and therefore the heat energy is not as easily transmitted.

Would you rather drink hot chocolate from an aluminum cup or from a china cup? Would you prefer a metal or a wooden handle for your frying pan?

HOW HEAT TRAVELS IN WATER AND AIR

1. Place some grains of sand, pieces of sawdust, or tiny bits of blotting paper in a jar. Fill the jar almost full of water and heat it in a pot of water. Feel or measure the temperature.

You will see that: As the water is heated, the hotter particles go to the top. The sand moves so as to show how the currents are travelling from bottom to top.

Explanation: When liquids are heated, they expand and take up more room. That means that they weigh less when warmed.

This warm, lighter part of the water moves upward while the heavier, cooler part sinks. The current in the experiment continues as long as there is a difference of temperature within.

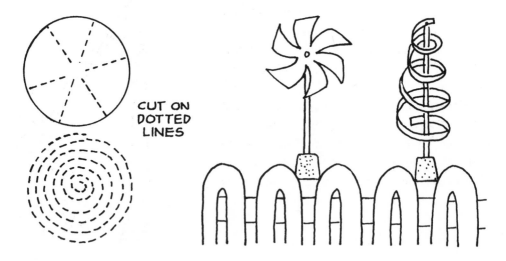

CUT ON
DOTTED
LINES

Now you can understand why furnaces are usually placed in the basement rather than in the attic.

2. From a milk carton or piece of cardboard, cut a pinwheel and spiral, as illustrated. Mount each on a knitting needle or wooden stick. Hold each above a hot radiator or lighted electric lamp.

You will see that: The pinwheel revolves. The spiral seems to rise.

Explanation: The gadgets are set in motion by air currents produced as the warm air rises and the cold air sinks. Wind is simply moving air.

HEATING BY RADIATION

Punch small holes on each side of a large tin can. Blacken the inside half of the can, where one hole is, with paint or soot from a candle flame. Insert used matchsticks in each hole. Melt wax and let it harden on the ends of the sticks. Hold a lighted bulb in the center of the can.

You will see that: The blackened side gets hotter; the wax on the matchstick on that side melts first.

Explanation: The dull black surface absorbs and radiates more heat than the bright shiny surface. Heat hitting the shiny surface is bounced back to the lamp; it is reflected.

The sun is not the only source of radiating heat. Everything radiates heat all the time. Do you see now why we wear light-colored clothes in the summer and dark clothes in the winter?

5. SOUND

WHAT CAUSES SOUND?

1. Attach one end of a clothesline or Venetian-blind cord to a doorknob. Measure off about 4 feet of line and rest your foot on the line so that a portion is kept taut. Pluck it.

2. Say "ah-h-h" as you touch the sides of your throat.

3. Place paper clips or bobby pins on a drum (you can make your own drum by encircling a coffee can with wrapping paper). Beat the drum top lightly.

4. Whisper "too" into straws of different lengths.

5. Strike a fork with another utensil and bring it close to your ear.

6. Hold a steel knitting needle or yardstick on the edge of a table. Pull the needle or yardstick upward and let it snap down quickly.

You will see that: In each case, you hear a sound—and you see or feel a movement to and fro.

Explanation: In each of your experiments, you make sound by causing an object to vibrate—to move back and forth or up and down. The number of vibrations per second (known as the frequency) depends on the size, shape and material of the object that is vibrating.

Our ears cannot hear sound unless the object vibrates at least 16 times per second and not more than 20,000 times per second. We know, however, that certain insects and birds can hear objects vibrating at a much faster speed. You can summon your dog with a special whistle which your dog can hear but you cannot because it vibrates so fast.

SEEING SOUND WAVES

Attach dry cereal kernels (such as puffed rice) to threads by gluing, sewing or by merely wrapping thread around each kernel. Suspend the threads (close to one another) from a clothes hanger. Hook the hanger onto the back of a chair or shelf so that you need not hold it. Then stretch a rubber band out from your clenched teeth and pluck the taut rubber band next to (but not touching) the kernel or ball in the center.

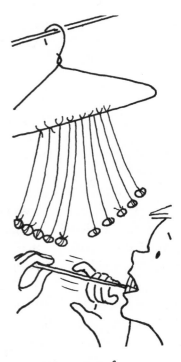

You will see that: The vibration of the rubber band causes the ball next to it to move. As the ball moves to and fro, it hits a ball on each side, which in turn hits its neighbors. This continues until the energy is spent. If the rubber band is plucked harder, more balls move. No one ball, however, moves very far.

Explanation: This will give you an idea of how sound travels from a vibrating object to your ear. When an object vibrates to make sound, the object bumps the small invisible air or solid or liquid particles or molecules next to it on all sides. Before they bounce back, the molecules bounce into other molecules near by. These bump into their own neighbors. Thus, while each molecule moves but slightly, sound may travel great distances. Finally, the molecules of your ear are bumped, your eardrum vibrates, the nerve endings take the vibrations to your brain and there they are converted to sound.

CAN SOUND TRAVEL THROUGH NOTHING?

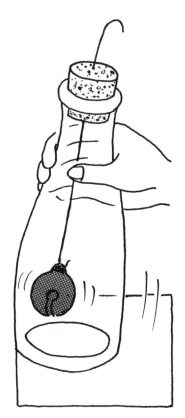

If there is no air to carry a wave from a vibrating object to our ears, can we hear a sound?

In this experiment you take the air out of an "empty" bottle to create a vacuum. Use a glass coffeepot or quart milk bottle fitted with a cork so that you can close it tightly. You'll also need a length of wire and a small bell or two. Thread the wire through the bell and attach it to the cork. Be sure the bell is free to ring without hitting the sides of the bottle when you shake it.

Tear a sheet of newspaper into shreds and put them into the bottle. Light a match and apply it to the paper. Quickly cover the bottle with the cork. The burning paper will use up the air and create a partial vacuum.

When the bottle cools, shake it and listen. Then open the cork and let in some air. Reseal the bottle and shake it again.

You will see that: After you remove most of the air, you are not able to hear the bell, though you see the clapper moving. When you let in the air, you hear the bell again.

Explanation: If sound is to travel from a vibrating object to your ear, there must be a substance to carry it. Sound cannot travel in a vacuum. Normally, the energy of sound travels in waves through the air. Though air is sound's most usual carrier, it is not its most effective.

CAN SOUND TRAVEL
THROUGH A LIQUID?

Click together two stones, two blocks, or two pot lids. Listen to the sound. Then submerge them in a basin of water—or take them into the bathtub with you—and listen to the sound they make under water.

You will see that: The sound in water is clearer, louder.

Explanation: Liquids carry sound farther and faster than air, as you may have been aware if you have ever heard sounds carry across a lake. In water, sound travels more than four times as fast as in air. Did you ever notice that sounds seem louder on foggy days than on clear days?

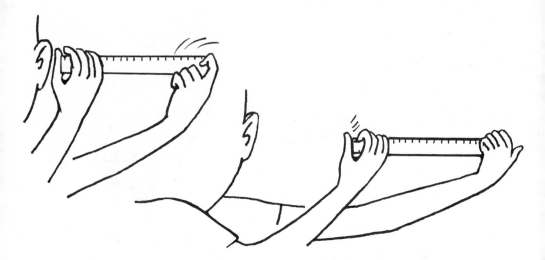

CAN SOUND TRAVEL THROUGH A SOLID?

Hold one end of a 12-inch ruler 1 inch from your ear and scratch on the far end of the ruler. Note how loud the sound is. Then move the ruler 13 inches away from your ear and scratch on the near end, so that you are making noise at the same distance from your ear as before. Compare the sound you hear.

You will see that: The sound is much louder when carried by the wooden ruler than by air.

Explanation: Many solids are much better carriers of sound than air or water. It is believed this is so because the molecules of a solid are closer together than those of either a gas or liquid.

Get a friend or neighbor to tap out a rhythm on a radiator or pipe from a floor above or below you. You will hear him very well. Metals are the best of all conductors of sound. In some, sound travels 16 times as fast as it does through air.

Indians and pioneer scouts knew that the solid earth is a better conductor of sound than air. They put their ears to the ground to hear distant sounds.

SPEED OF SOUND

During the next thunderstorm in your area, you can have fun with this activity.

When you see a flash of lightning, start counting and continue until you hear the roar of thunder. Divide the number you get by 5. This will give you a rough estimate of the number of miles away the center of the storm is.

Explanation: Sound takes about 5 seconds to travel a mile in air. (It travels about 1,100 feet a second, and there are 5,280 feet in a mile.) Light, on the other hand, takes only a small fraction of a second to travel a mile. (It travels 186,000 miles per second.) The lightning and thunder occur at the same time but travel to us at different speeds. This accounts for the different times they reach us.

Variation: If you're too impatient to wait for a thunderstorm, you can set up a similar experiment. Ask a friend to play a drum some distance from you, so that you can both watch and listen. Or watch your friend batting from far away on the baseball field. Notice there is a time lag between the time you see him hit the drum or ball and the time you hear the sound.

ECHOES

Here's an experiment you can perform in a large empty gym or auditorium. It's also a perfect activity when you're hiking in the country or the mountains. You can judge the distance from one side of the gym to the other, or how far you are from a cliff, barn or from a bridge overhead.

Note your position and shout out a message. Then count the number

of seconds it takes before you hear an echo and divide this by 2, then by 5. This gives you the distance in miles. The sound travels to the cliff and back to you so you divide by 2. Because sound travels ⅕ of a mile per second in air, you divide by 5.

If your echo returns within 4 seconds, for example, the cliff is about ⅖ of a mile away.

Explanation: When sound waves hit a solid object, some pass through, but some bounce back like a ball. The reflected sound is heard as a separate sound (or echo) if the distance is 40 feet or more. The human ear requires at least 1/15 of a second to hear separate sounds. Sound travels at about 1,100 feet per second, so it takes about 1/15 of a second to travel a distance of 40 feet and back.

The depth of water is measured on shipboard in the same way. Sound, however, travels faster in salt water—4,800 feet per second.

CONTROLLING THE DIRECTION OF SOUND

Sound waves travel out in all directions from the source of sound. But, we can concentrate sound energy in one direction, instead of permitting it to spread. Using equipment around the house, you can see how a few of these devices for concentrating sound operate.

MEGAPHONE

Make a simple megaphone from a sheet of paper or from cardboard. Fold as in the illustration.

Have someone speak into the narrow end while you listen from a distance. Listen to the ticking of a watch at the narrow end while you stand a few feet away.

SPEAKING TUBE

All you need for this device is an old garden hose. You can convert it into an excellent speaking tube merely by patching any holes and making sure both ends are open. Take turns with a friend, talking and listening. You will be able to speak back and forth over a considerable distance because the sound is being channelled directly to your ears by the air inside the hose. Many ships still use speaking tubes for communicating on board.

STETHOSCOPE

Attach rubber tubing, perhaps an old shower hose, to the kind of funnel used to fill bottles with liquid. Then use your homemade stethoscope as your doctor does his. Put the end of the tube in your ear and listen to the beat of your own heart.

The funnel and tube concentrate the sound and therefore it is made louder.

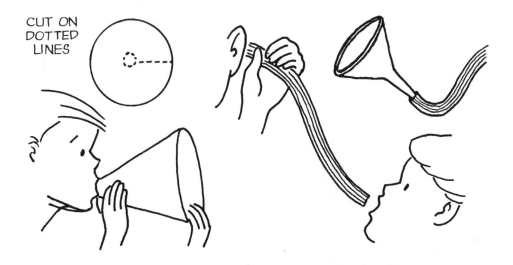

CUT ON DOTTED LINES

SOUND DIFFERENCES: PITCH

Pitch is the highness or lowness of a sound.

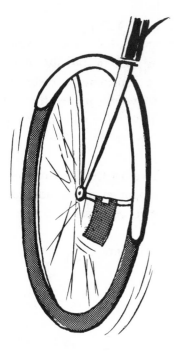

1. Hold the edge of a card against a bicycle wheel. Revolve the wheel slowly and then gradually faster and faster.

Note how the sound changes.

2. Play a 33 r.p.m. phonograph record at the different speeds on a 3-speed phonograph. Notice what happens to the shrillness of the sound.

You will see that: The faster you spin the bicycle wheel, the higher the sound will become. Similarly, the faster the phonograph revolves, the higher the sound.

Explanation: Pitch depends on the number of vibrations per second. The more vibrations, the higher the pitch.

VARIATIONS WITH STRINGS

String four rubber bands of various thicknesses around a rectangular cereal box. Make a bridge from a thin block or piece of plywood. Place it as in the illustration. Now you have a box banjo.

Pluck each of the strings in turn and compare sounds.

Now shorten the rubber bands by moving the bridge. Is the sound lower or higher than with the longer band?

Insert a thumbtack on the far side of the box. Use this to stretch one band tighter and tighter as you pluck.

You will see that: The thinnest band produces the highest note; the thickest, the lowest. The shorter the band, the higher the note; the tighter you stretch the band, the higher the note you get.

Explanation: The pitch depends on the tension, length and thickness of a band or string.

In general, the smaller the vibrating surface, the faster the vibrations and the higher the pitch. For instance, the thin band will produce a higher note than a thick one of same length because the thick band has a larger surface and produces slower vibrations. It has more molecules to set in motion than the thinner one.

STRIKING SOUNDS

Take a handful of long wooden blocks and a jump rope. Also get two pencils and two empty spools. Make mallets by fitting together the pencils and spools.

Then shape your rope in the form of a horseshoe. Arrange your blocks on top of the rope so that the shortest is centered on the narrow ends and the longest is centered on the wide part of the horseshoe. Each block should overhang the rope on each side ¼ of its length so that it is free to vibrate.

You will see that: You have made a ladder of sound, ranging from the low-sounding long block to the high-sounding short block.

Explanation: The pitch depends on the number of vibrations per second. The smaller surface can vibrate faster and therefore makes a higher sound.

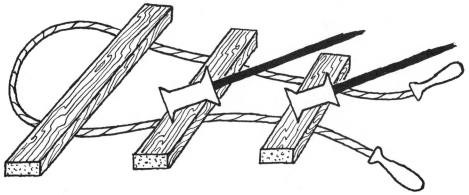

BLOWING SOUNDS

Press the top edge of an empty bottle to your lower lip and blow lightly across the top.

Pour in a little water and blow again. Then add more water and blow.

You will see that: The more water you add, the higher your sound will be.

Explanation: You are vibrating the air in the bottle. When you add water you leave less room for air. The less air there is in the bottle, the faster it vibrates and the higher the sound. In the same way the higher notes on a musical instrument are made by shortening the air column. In general, the larger the instrument, the lower the notes it can play and the smaller the instrument, the higher the notes it can play.

LOUDNESS

The loudness of a sound depends not on the speed of the vibrations but on the energy of the vibrations. Demonstrate this for yourself with the following activities:

1. Clap hands gently—and then vigorously.

2. Hold one end of a ruler over the edge of the table. Pull the other end down gently and then let go. Listen to the sound. Repeat with a harder pull.

You will see that: The more energy you apply, the louder the sound is. The louder the sound, the farther the body vibrates.

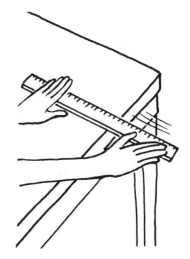

Explanation: More energy causes the molecules of air over a greater distance to be moved back and forth.

AMPLIFYING LOUDNESS

Strike the prongs of a fork in mid-air with a spoon. Listen to the sound. Repeat—but this time quickly press the handle of the fork to the table, holding the fork upright. Notice the difference in loudness.

You will see that: Touching the vibrating fork to the table makes the sound considerably louder.

Explanation: Sounds can be made louder if other objects vibrate too. Ordinarily, the larger the vibrating surface, the louder the sound. Many musical instruments have wood or metal sounding boards or boxes to make the sound louder.

WHAT IS RESONANCE?

Two milk or soda bottles will demonstrate resonance (or sympathetic vibration) for you and a friend.

Hold one of the bottles to your ear while your friend blows across the mouth of the second bottle until he produces a clear note.

You will see that: Your bottle will vibrate in sympathy and sound a similar, though weaker, note.

Explanation: Each object has a natural rate of vibration, depending on its nature, its size and shape. When two objects naturally vibrate at the same rate, one object can make the other vibrate. The two are said to be in resonance.

Strike A on a piano and watch a nearby violin. It will vibrate sympathetically.

Did you know that soldiers crossing a bridge deliberately march out of step? If their steps in unison should happen to match the natural rate of vibration of the bridge, it would set the bridge in violent motion, and this might destroy it.

SEASHELL RESONANCE

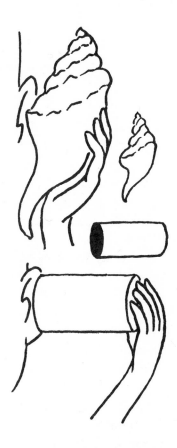

A couple of seashells and two open cans serve as the equipment for this experiment.

Choose a large and a small shell and put each in turn to your ear. Do you hear any difference in sound?

Now put a large and a small can, in turn, to your ear.

Vary the setting for the experiment from indoors to outdoors, from beach to city street.

You will see that: You hear bass sounds from the large shell and high sounds from the small shell. You hear low sounds from the large can and soprano sounds from the small can. The sounds indoors differ from outdoors; beach differs from city.

Explanation: Of course, the sounds coming from the seashells are not the "sounds of the sea." They are sympathetic vibrations. The enclosed air in the shell vibrates in response to those sounds in the outside air that correspond to the pitch of the shell. The particular rate of vibration depends on shape, type of material, and amount of air enclosed.

6. LIGHT

We need light to see—natural light from the sun, or artificial light from a match, a candle, a lamp.

Like heat, sound and electricity, light is a form of energy; it is capable of doing work.

Anything will give off light if it can be heated enough before it changes to another substance. It is believed that the heat excites the atoms of a material, and that some of the electrons of the atom jump out of place. When the electrons jump back into their normal place, bundles of energy shoot out. These bundles are sometimes called photons. A line of these photons forms a ray of light; a group of rays forms a beam of light. Photons travel from all light-giving objects, strike the eye, and cause us to see light.

Another way scientists explain light is by the wave theory. It is believed that light is sent out in the form of waves, similar to water waves. Light waves are very short, about 1/50,000 of an inch.

Unlike sound, light can travel in a vacuum, in empty space where there is not even air. Light travels at a speed of 186,000 miles per second, the fastest speed known to man.

CAN WE SEE IN THE DARK?

Make a pinhole in the side of a shoe box or any box that can be closed tightly. Put a ball and a pencil in the box. Cover the box and look through the pinhole. Do you see the ball or the pencil? Do you see anything?

Take off the cover of the box. Look through the pinhole again. Do you see anything?

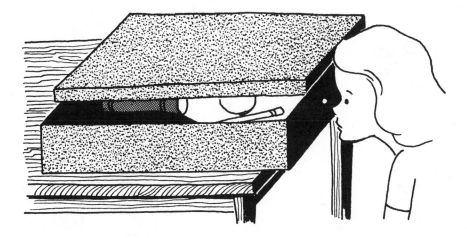

You will see that: You cannot see the pencil and ball when the cover is on and you can see both when the cover is off. With the lighted flashlight inside, you can see flashlight, ball and pencil.

Explanation: Without a source of light (such as the sun or the flashlight) you cannot see. You cannot make out either shape or color.

Light comes to our eyes in two ways. Light from the sun or the flashlight or other *luminous* objects comes directly to our eyes. This is how we see the stars, lightning, an electric bulb, a match or a candle.

But we cannot see a ball or a pencil directly. Light from the flashlight hits the ball and bounces back (is reflected) to our eyes. We see people, chairs, trees because light is bounced off them.

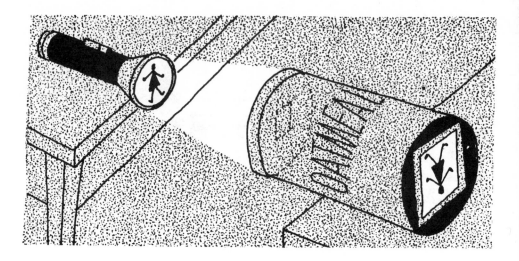

A PINHOLE CAMERA

Cut an opening about 3 inches square out of the bottom of a round cereal box. Over this hole, paste very thin paper (tissue paper or onionskin). Cut another square hole, about the size of a small postage stamp, in the center of the top of the box. Cover this with tinfoil. In the center of the tinfoil make a small hole with a pin.

Cut out a paper doll and crayon it black. Tape the doll with cellophane tape to the glass of a flashlight.

Hold the box about 2 feet away from the lighted lamp (preferably in a darkened room). Point the pinhole at the lamp and look at the tissue paper.

You will see: An image of the doll is thrown on the tissue paper—upside down.

Explanation: The rays of light travel in straight lines from the lamp to the image, as shown in the illustration. This is what happens in our eye. The image forms upside down on the retina at the back of the eye. Our brain turns the image right side up again.

DUST HELPS US TO SEE

Arrange your window shades so that only a small ray of bright sunshine comes into the room. Follow the beam of light with your eye.

You will see that: You can see dust moving in the path of the ray of light.

Explanation: Dust particles bounce back (reflect) light and help us to see indoors and in other places where the sun does not shine directly.

Without dust, we would not have daylight inside our house except when we received the direct rays of the sun.

HOW LIGHT BOUNCES

In a dark room, place a mirror on the floor. Cast a beam from a flashlight directly down to the mirror. Sprinkle talcum powder or chalk dust near the beam. Follow the reflection on the ceiling.

Then slant your flashlight and cast a slanting beam at your mirror. Observe the reflection.

You will see that: The beam that travels straight down to the mirror bounces back straight up to the ceiling. The beam that travels on a slant down to the mirror bounces back on an opposite slant to the wall.

Explanation: A ray of light striking a surface is reflected at the same angle.

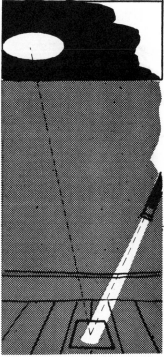

HOW DO YOU REALLY LOOK?

Stand up two pocket mirrors and tape them together so that they form a right angle, as in the illustration. Face a clock toward the two mirrors. Try to read this page in the mirrors. Look at yourself. Try to comb your hair.

You will see that: You can read the clock and the book. You look strange and you can't seem to comb the side of the hair you mean to.

Explanation: Light from the left side of your face hits the left mirror and is reflected to the right-hand mirror, which reflects it back to your eye. The same thing happens on the other side of your face. Thus you see yourself as others see you, instead of the way you usually look in the mirror.

MAKE A PERISCOPE

Use a milk carton or make a cardboard or wooden box about that size.

Cut a hole on one side of the box, near the top, and a similar hole on the opposite side, the same distance from the bottom. Tape two pocket mirrors in place parallel to one another, at a 45-degree slant, as in the illustration.

Hold the box up to your eye and look through the lower hole. Now go to a corner and hold the box so that one hole is sticking out. Look through the other hole. What do you see?

MIRRORS AT 45° ANGLE

You will see that: You can see what is above you and on the opposite side of the box. You can also see around corners.

Explanation: Light is reflected by the mirror on top of the periscope to the mirror on the bottom. An object facing the top hole can be seen through the bottom hole.

Periscopes are used in submarines to see above water. In some parts of the world, theatres are equipped with periscopes so that you can see the stage even if the person in front is taller than you.

BENDING LIGHT RAYS

Place a pencil, a ruler or a spoon in half a glass of water. Look at it from the top, bottom and sides.

You will see that: When you look at the pencil from the side, the pencil appears to be bent or broken at the point where it enters the water.

Explanation: The light rays appear to be bent because the speed at which they travel in the thicker water is slower than in air. Light travels in air at the high speed of 186,000 miles per second. It travels ¾ of that speed in water. The bending of light is known as refraction.

READING GLASS

Pour water into a clean glass or jar. Hold it close to this page and read through the side of the glass.

You will find that: The print appears larger.

Explanation: Because the glass is curved, the light rays enter it on a slant and change direction as they go through the water. This is how a magnifying lens works.

WHAT CAUSES A SHADOW?

In a darkened room, shine a strong flashlight or a shaded lamp bulb on a white wall, or on a sheet tacked to the wall, as in the illustration. Place the lamp 5 to 10 feet from the wall.

Stand *behind* the lamp. Do you make a shadow?

Hold up your hand, or stand *between* the lamp and the wall. What happens? Move farther away from the light and closer to the wall. What happens to the shadow?

You will see that: You do not cast a shadow when you stand behind the light. You cast a big shadow when you stand near the light and far from the wall. As you move farther from the light, the shadow becomes smaller.

Explanation: You cast a shadow by blocking the rays of light. As you move away from the source of light, your shadow becomes smaller because you cut off fewer of the light rays. Any object that won't permit light to pass through creates a shadow, an area of lessened light.

MAKING RAINBOWS

1. Stand a glass of water on a window ledge in bright sunlight. Place a sheet of white paper on the floor. What do you see on the paper?

2. Set a tray of water in bright sunlight. Rest a mirror upright against one edge of the tray. Look at the wall.

3. In a darkened room, hold a prism (a 3-sided piece of glass), a crystal doorknob, a cut-glass bottle or even a milk bottle up to the sun or another source of light, such as a lamp bulb or flashlight. Look at the wall, ceiling or floor.

You will see that: You see the colors of the rainbow.

Explanation: You are separating the various colors (the spectrum) that make up white light. When the light passes at a slant from the air through the glass or water, the rays change direction. They are refracted. The different colors are bent differently: violet is bent the most and red the least. When the light comes out of the glass or water, the different colors travel in slightly different directions and strike the screen at different places.

Rainbows in the sky are made when sunlight shines through water drops in the air. The water drops bend the sun's rays to form a spectrum.

MAGIC COLORS

1. With water colors or poster paints, color one side of a cardboard disk red and the other side blue. Punch small holes on opposite sides of the disk, as in the illustration. Thread short lengths of string through each hole.

Hold the cardboard by its strings and twirl it around.

You will see that: The color you see is purple.

2. Make a toy top by dividing a cardboard disk into alternating segments of blue and yellow. Thread a string through a hole in the center, as in the illustration. Then spin the disk.

You will find that: The color you see is green.

Explanation: The disk reflects both colors. You see a third color when your eye and your brain mix the colors of the rapidly whirling disks. This happens because the eye continues to see each color for a short time after it has disappeared.

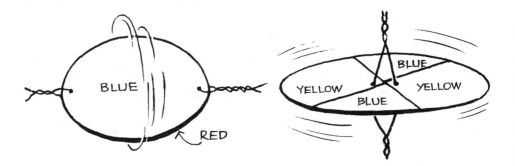

7. MAGNETISM AND ELECTRICITY

Both electricity and magnetism were known more than 2500 years ago. But it was not until the beginning of the 19th century, about 150 years ago, that experiments showed a definite connection between the two.

In 1819, Hans Oersted showed that electricity can produce magnetism. A few years later, in 1831, Michael Faraday proved that magnets can make electricity.

From these experiments and those that followed came our modern electrical world—telegraph, doorbell, telephone, electric motor, generator, radio and television. We use magnets to produce the electricity that lights our homes and factories.

We have put magnetism and electricity to work for us. We are not sure, however, what causes either form of energy. We are still trying to figure out *why* they work.

WHAT DOES A MAGNET DO?

You will need a magnet—in the shape of a bar, U or horseshoe. A ten-cent toy magnet will do.

Jumble together a box of paper clips, pins or small nails with a collection of buttons or pennies. Use the magnet to separate the items.

You will see that: The objects made of iron or steel are drawn to the magnet. If your magnet is a strong one, some will even jump up to it. The plastic buttons and copper pennies do not move, nor do pins of brass.

Explanation: A magnet is an object that attracts iron and steel and certain alloys. A few other metals—cobalt, nickel, aluminum and platinum—can also be attracted but only by much more powerful magnets.

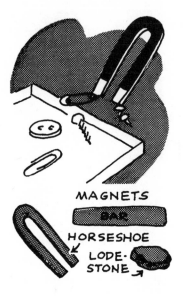

Natural magnets are a form of iron ore called "magnetite," or "lodestone" meaning "leading stone." Man-made magnets, such as the horseshoe or bar you use, are usually either iron or steel. Very strong magnets are made of an iron alloy called alnico, which contains aluminum, nickel and cobalt.

MAGNETS

BAR

HORSESHOE

LODE-
STONE

CAN MAGNETS ATTRACT THROUGH SUBSTANCES?

Assemble tacks, nails and clips. Then, with your magnet, try to attract the various items in the following ways:

1. Put several clips into an empty, dry drinking-glass. Move the magnet about underneath the glass.

2. Put some tacks or nails on the table and cover them with a sheet of paper. Move your horseshoe magnet slowly over the paper.

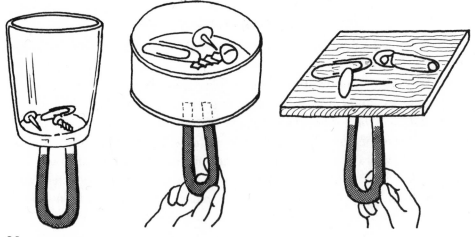

3. Put brads (headless nails) into a dish of water. Place a magnet just above the water.

4. Put several nails into a "tin" can. Move the magnet about beneath the can.

5. Put a clip on top of a thin piece of wood, leather, rubber or cork. Move the magnet around slowly underneath.

You will see that: Magnets can act through glass, plastic, water, paper, leather, rubber and cork—but *not* through the can which is really an iron can coated with tin.

Explanation: Magnets can act through most substances. Iron and steel and other highly magnetic materials, however, take up the magnetism themselves and prevent the power from passing through.

WHERE IS A MAGNET THE STRONGEST?

Lower a magnet of any type into a pile of nails or clips or pins. Try picking up the nails with the different parts of the magnet.

You will see that: The nails cling to the ends of the magnet.

Explanation: A magnet has the strongest attraction at its ends. These are known as the north and south poles of the magnet. In the horseshoe, or U magnet, the bar has been bent so that the poles or strongest parts are close together. This increases its lifting power.

WHAT IS A SPARK?

Rub a comb with a piece of wool or fur. Hold it near a water tap, metal radiator or doorknob.

You will see that: You will produce a small spark.

Explanation: By rubbing the comb, you charge it with electricity. The spark is made when the charge jumps to the uncharged (or neutral) tap. A spark is the passage of an electrical charge between two objects.

You may have seen a similar spark when you rubbed your shoes on a rug and then touched something. Or you may have heard a crackling while combing your hair. These are examples of static electricity.

Lightning is a huge electric spark that results when charges jump from one cloud to another or from a cloud to the ground.

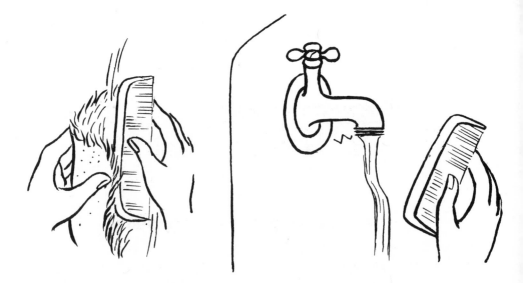

ELECTRICITY CAN ATTRACT

Turn on the water faucet so that you get a fine, even stream of water. Rub a glass straw with a piece of silk or a comb with a piece of wool or fur. Hold the straw or comb near the stream of water.

You will see that: The stream bends toward the charged glass or comb.

Explanation: The charged object attracts the neutral stream of water.

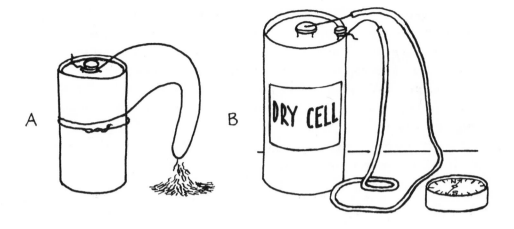

A B

ELECTRICITY PRODUCES MAGNETISM

Now you are going to produce magnetic effects without a magnet.

Your equipment will include iron filings, a strip of heavy copper wire, a 3-foot length of covered (insulated) bell wire, a compass, and a dry cell battery. A flashlight battery will serve instead of a larger dry cell, if you make a holder for it or strip off the outer cardboard.

1. Connect the ends of the bare copper wire to the cell or battery as in illustration A. Dip a loop of the wire into the iron filings. Then quickly disconnect one end of the wire so that you don't wear out the battery.

You will see that: The iron filings stick to the wire. When you disconnect one end of the wire and stop the flow of electricity, the filings soon drop off.

2. Scrape the covering from the ends of the 3-foot length of covered wire. Substitute this for the bare wire, arranging it so that one length is vertical as in illustration B, but don't attach one end. Place the compass at the side of the wire. Rearrange the battery and wires so that the needle is pointing toward the wire. Attach the loose end of the wire to the battery and note the results. Disconnect the wire at both ends, and reconnect them

to the opposite posts, to reverse the direction of the electric current. Then observe the needle.

You will see that: The compass needle moves first in one direction and then, when the current is reversed, in the opposite direction.

Explanation: When electricity flows through a wire, the wire acts like a magnet and produces a magnetic field. The magnetism lasts only while the current is flowing.

This was Oersted's significant discovery of 1819. A wire carrying a current of electricity produces magnetism.

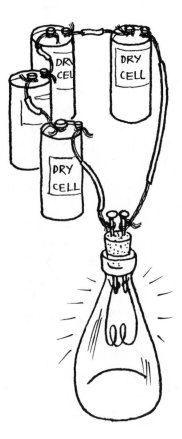

MAKING AN ELECTRIC LAMP

You can make your own electric lamp and get a bright, though brief, glow. You'll need two nails, a short length of thin iron wire (a strand of picture frame wire), an ordinary bottle or jar, a cork to fit the bottle, and about four dry cell batteries with a length of covered copper wire.

Stick the two nails through the cork. Attach the iron wire to the nail points. Fit the cork into the neck of the bottle, allowing the nailheads to remain outside and the iron wire to go inside. With the covered wire, connect the dry cells to the heads of the nails, as shown in the illustration.

You will see that: The thin iron wire gets hot enough to glow and you have made an electric lamp of the bottle. Soon, however, the iron wire gets so hot that it burns in the air of the bottle. The iron breaks and the lamp goes out.

Explanation: In our modern electric lamp, nitrogen (which doesn't support burning) is substituted for the air within the bulb. Tungsten is used for the inner (filament) wire because this metal can get white hot and glow without melting. Since it requires less heat to make a thin wire glow, an extremely thin tungsten wire is used.

CONDUCTORS AND INSULATORS

Connect a dry cell to a flashlight bulb and socket, leaving two bare ends of copper wire, as shown in the illustration. Briefly touch these ends together to make sure that the bulb lights. You now have a tester with which you can find out whether certain materials allow electricity to flow.

Touch the two bare ends of wire to two points on any of the following objects you have available: a clip, fork, key, coin, piece of cloth, wood, glass, rubber band, leather heel, nails, pins, paper, chalk, covered wire.

You can also try a number of solutions: salted water, lemon juice, vinegar. (You may need more than one battery to provide the current for these.)

Also try different kinds of wire—copper, iron, aluminum.

You will see that: Metals are generally good conductors and will light

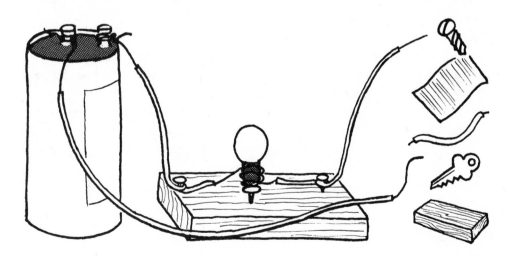

the bulb. Non-metals will not conduct electric current. (They are called "insulators.") Solutions made with salts, acids or alkalies will conduct. Notice that the various kinds of wire differ in effectiveness. The lamp burns brightest with the copper wire.

Explanation: In producing static electricity, we used insulating materials such as glass and rubber which do not permit electricity to move freely. These insulators are valuable in helping us keep electricity from going where it is not wanted. This is why we cover wire with rubber, cloth or thread. Electricity will flow only if it makes the return trip to its source; it flows in a circuit. When we want electricity to move along a path, or circuit, we use conductors.

ELECTRICITY CAN PRODUCE HEAT

You know from your toaster, heater, iron, electric stove, and other electrical devices that electricity can be used to produce heat. If you would like to do your own changing of electrical energy to heat, you can try this simple experiment.

Use a short length of thin bare iron wire—one thin strand of picture frame wire will do. Connect one end to a dry cell. Then wrap the other end around a pencil and hold it to the other cell terminal, as in the illustration.

You will see that: The wire will get red hot and possibly even break if you don't disconnect it in time.

Explanation: Different kinds of wire act differently when electricity flows through them. The iron wire that we used in the experiment gets hot because it resists electric current. It does not conduct as well as copper or aluminum but instead changes the energy to heat. When the same current flows through two wires, the wire with the greater resistance to electricity gets hotter.

Thicker wire permits a larger current, for thin wire has more resistance than thick. Similarly, a long wire allows less of the current being applied to flow than a short wire does.

Heating elements in toasters and irons are made of alloys with a higher resistance than the copper wire in the insulated cord.

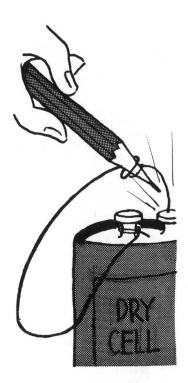

INDEX

ACKNOWLEDGMENT

The author wishes to thank physicist Irving Lazar for his technical help.